W
MA

CW00344987

Published by RDG
Cotswold Business Village
Moreton-in-Marsh
Gloucestershire
GL56 0JQ
United Kingdom

*A catalogue record for this book is available
from the British Library.*

Designed by
the workshop, Longhope,
Gloucestershire

Printed in China

ISBN: 1-903680-04-2

If you're in charge
and you stop rowing,

don't be surprised
  if the rest of your crew
stops as well.

It isn't
the employees
you terminate
that make
your life
miserable,
*it's the ones
you **don't**.*

It is a very
special person
who wants to hear
what he doesn't
want to hear.

There are many
keys to success,
but one sure key
to failure is
trying to *please
everybody*
all of the time.

*Only make a great deal
if you have no intention
of doing business with
that person again;
otherwise make a good deal.*

IF THERE ARE THINGS
ABOUT A JOB CANDIDATE
THAT YOU DON'T LIKE,
YOU'LL LIKE THEM
EVEN LESS AFTER
YOU HAVE HIRED THEM.

Dumb executives tend to become best friends with other dumb executives.

If you're business
isn't moving
fast enough,
consider the turtle,

**it can't move
at all if it
doesn't stick
it's neck out.**

*The executive
who works
from 8 till 8 every day
will be very successful
and fondly remembered
by his partner's
next partner.*

IN BUSINESS TODAY,
TOO MANY EXECUTIVES
SPEND MONEY
THEY HAVE EARNED
TO BUY THINGS
THEY DON'T NEED
TO IMPRESS PEOPLE
THEY DON'T EVEN LIKE.

*People
who will lie
for you
will lie
to you.*

If your business
is stupid enough
to be run by
a committee,
make sure
you're on
that committee.

The executive who doesn't make any mistakes usually doesn't make anything.

In business as in life,
foolish ideas dressed up
to look impressive
*are usually dreamed up
by impressive fools.*

WISE WORDS
FOR MANAGERS

A **fat** lawsuit is never as smart as a lean compromise.

If your only choice
is to hire either a conceited
or foolish individual,
hire the conceited one;
occasionally he or she
won't be conceited.

AVOID SHORTCUTS,
they always take too much time in the long run.

LEARN FROM THE MISTAKES OF OTHERS;

you won't live long enough to make them all yourself.

If you want something done, ask a busy person.

You can't build a reputation
on what you are going to do,
but on
what you do do.

There are those that make things happen,

there are those that watch things happen

and there are those who wonder **what** happened.

A truly great discovery is when one learns we can alter our lives by altering our attitudes.

THE WAY TO GET STARTED IS TO QUIT TALKING AND START DOING.

NO WORK TAKES PLACE AT A MEETING

as most of the time is spent talking about what the attendees should already be doing.

Most people think of changing the world,
but very few think of changing themselves.

CHANGE
MAY
NOT
TAKE
TIME,
but it does take
COMMITMENT.

It is not the employer
who pays the wages -
employers only
launder the money -
it is the CUSTOMERS
who pay the wages.

Attentiveness is one of the greatest gifts you can give someone.

The person
who gets ahead
is the one
who does more
than is necessary
and
keeps on doing it.

PRACTICE DOES NOT MAKE PERFECT, PERFECT PRACTICE MAKES PERFECT.

One of life's little ironies
is that when you finally
master a tough job, **YOU
MAKE
IT LOOK
EASY.**

If **you** want to cheer up - cheer somebody **else** up.

PROBABLY THE
GREATEST OF
ALL FAULTS IS
TO BE CONSCIOUS
OF NONE.

Some people dread fear so much that they eliminate any risk at all.

An expert is a person
who will know
TOMORROW
why the things
he predicted
YESTERDAY
didn't happen
TODAY.

A person persuaded against his will retains the same opinion still.

DO ACCEPT,

THE MORE WE DO SOMETHING GOOD
THE LESS PRAISE WE GET FOR IT,
THE MORE WE DO SOMETHING BAD
THE MORE PUNISHMENT WE RECEIVE.

It is more important to do the right things than to do things right.

If they
gave a
reward
for
finding
fault,
some
people
would
get
rich
quick.

INSINCERE PRAISE IS WORSE THAN NO PRAISE AT ALL.

NO PERSON WHO DOES
NOT FEEL GENUINE JOY
AT THE SUCCESS OF THOSE
UNDER THEM OR THOSE
WHO HAVE BEEN UNDER THEM
WILL EVER BE A GREAT LEADER.

If you DON'T give people

INFORMATION

they will make up something to fill the void.

An
untreated
complaint
is like an
untreated
wound,
it festers &
gets worse.

A leader's worst decision can be the one that is not made

If you want
to be more
successful,
make or help
someone else
to be more
successful.

WHATEVER
YOU HAND
OUT IN LIFE
YOU WILL
GET BACK,
SO BE CAREFUL
WHAT YOU
DISH OUT.

LEAD BY EXAMPLE, JUDGE BY RESULTS.

Every person
is self-made
but only the
successful ones
admit it.

Formal education
        gets us our first job;
self education
        earns us our living.

Leadership
is the ability to
get people to do
what they don't normally
want to do and then
like it.

IF YOU WERE GOING ON HOLIDAY **TOMORROW** WHAT WOULD YOU BE DOING **TODAY?**

Those who can't laugh at themselves *leave the job to others.*

Don't try to do something cheaply that shouldn't be done at all.

If someone
says something
unkind about you,
live your life
so that no-one
will believe it.

It does not
matter what
anybody else
says,
thinks,
or does - **it's what
you do
that really
matters.**

It's not whether
you get knocked down
that's important,
it's whether you
get up again.

THE FINEST WAY TO ELIMINATE AN ENEMY IS TO MAKE HIM A FRIEND.

BEWARE

of the most dangerous person in business,
the articulate incompetent.

If you keep doing
what you are doing,
you'll keep getting
what you are getting.

NEVER UNDERESTIMATE THE IMPORTANCE OF MONEY,

it's how business people keep the score.

Don't be afraid to say,

I don't know –

people will respect you
much more and will
always place more weight
on what you do say,
because they know
you are right.

Don't keep the credit, share it -
people will work with you
and for you if they are recognised;
they will work against you
if they are not.

THERE ARE TWO TYPES OF FOOLS,

those who trust everyone

those who trust no–one.

Try not to work for a person who has **more problems** than you do.

Smart people know that they do the things they need to do when they need to do them so someday they can do the things they want to do when they want to do them.

NOTHING IS MORE REWARDING

THAN TO WATCH SOMEONE

WHO SAYS IT CAN'T BE DONE

GET INTERRUPTED BY SOMEONE

ACTUALLY DOING IT.

SPEND SOME EXTRA MONEY TO MAINTAIN YOUR EQUIPMENT–

remember you don't have to brush all your teeth either, only the ones you want to keep.

SPEAK

when you are angry
and you will make
the best speech
you will ever regret.

AGGRESSIVE behaviour

is most often motivated by fear;

assertive behaviour is most often motivated

by confidence.

THERE IS NOT A RIGHT WAY TO DO A WRONG THING

Isn't luck extraordinary; the harder you work, it seems the more you have of it.

A professional
is someone
who can do
his best work
when he
doesn't feel
like it.

When you can
think of yesterday
without regret
and a tomorrow
without fear,
then you are
on the road
to success.

*Never get so busy
making a living
that you forget
to make a* **LIFE**.

HE WHO CANNOT FORGIVE OTHERS DESTROYS THE BRIDGE OVER WHICH HE HIMSELF MUST PASS.

Be careful with the
people with whom you
share your goals because
they will play a major
part in whether or not
you reach your goals.

You can earn more money, but when time is spent it is gone forever.

It seems extraordinarily true
that people who have direction
in their lives go farther and faster
and get more done
in all areas of their lives.

*Most people who fail
in their dream
fail not from lack of ability
but lack of commitment.*

LAUGHTER

is good for business;

it can reduce stress,
enliven meetings
and spur creativity.

*Motivation is the fuel
that gives you the 'want to'
and gives you the strength,
character and commitment
to keep you going when the
going gets tough.*

One of the
best ways
to get ahead
is to teach
and help
the person
below you
how to
get ahead.

INTEGRITY
is a key ingredient to success, without integrity no-one listens and without trust no-one follows.

All of us
perform better
and more willingly
when we know *why*
we are doing
what we have been
told or asked to do.

People of genius   are **admired,**

people of wealth   are **envied,**

people of power   are **feared,**

people of **character** are **trusted.**

Surely
it's not
important
where you
start;
it's where
you finish
that counts.

YOU CAN PREACH A BETTER SERMON WITH YOUR LIFE THAN WITH YOUR LIPS.

One example
of *good manners*
is to be able to
put up pleasantly
with those who
demonstrate
bad manners.

*People who make
the worst use of time
often are the same ones
who complain that
there is never
enough time.*

When you look
in the mirror
you are looking
at the problem,
but remember
you are also looking
at the solution.

It's not **what** you say,
but **how** you say it,
hat will cause a reaction
or a response.

The key to willpower is to want power –

people who want something badly enough can usually find the willpower to achieve it.

PERHAPS ONCE
IN A HUNDRED YEARS
A PERSON MAY BE RUINED
BY EXCESSIVE PRAISE,
BUT SURELY ONCE
EVERY MINUTE
SOMEONE DIES
FOR LACK OF IT.

SO MUCH
OF WHAT IS CALLED
MANAGEMENT CONSISTS
OF MAKING IT DIFFICULT
FOR PEOPLE TO WORK
AND BE EFFECTIVE.

Your
temper
is one
of your
more
valuable
possessions –
**don't
lose it.**

If a cluttered desk
is a sign of a cluttered mind,
what then is an empty desk
a sign of?

NO MONUMENT HAS EVER BEEN ERECTED TO A CRITIC; MONUMENTS ARE ERECTED TO THOSE THAT GET CRITICISED.

You can never do a kindness
too soon
because you never know
how soon
it will be too late.

YES you can make some money giving people what they need, but you make serious money when you give them what they want.

The six P's of achievement – *proper*

planning

prevents

particularly

poor

performance.

The right suit
might get you
into the boardroom,
but the wrong one
will keep you OUT.

*In endeavouring
to select
one word
that would make
a good manager,
how about* decisiveness?

*The purpose of the body
is almost as a brain transporter.
If you don't take care of your body,
where else are you going to live?*

Isn't it really a rather sad truth of life that people will pay more to be entertained than educated - **invest a little in yourself.**

is said that

>> to be persuasive
>> one must be believable,
>> to be believable
>> one must be credible
>> and to be credible
>> one must be
>> **truthful**.

ONE THING YOU CAN GIVE AND STILL KEEP IS YOUR WORD.

THE
TOUGHEST
PART OF
CLIMBING
THE LADDER
OF SUCCESS
IS GETTING
THROUGH
THE CROWD
AT THE BOTTOM,
THE HIGHER
ONE GOES,
THE LESS
THERE ARE
IN THE WAY.

The way employees treat customers often reflects the manner in which they are being treated by management.

PASSION

**IS A FANTASTIC WORD,
IT IS IRRESISTIBLE,
IT IS SO POWERFUL,
IT IS ALSO SO PERSUASIVE.**

There is a big difference
in taking one's work seriously
and taking oneself seriously

The first is
imperative
and the second can
be **disastrous**.

An effective leader
is not someone
who is loved or necessarily admired,
it's someone whose followers
do the right things.
**POPULARITY IS
NOT LEADERSHIP,
RESULTS ARE.**

The more people
feel needed
on the job
the more
they are likely
to be **there**
and **on time**.

*The only way to live happily with people is to overlook their **faults** and admire their **virtues**.*

MOTIVATION
IS
EVERYTHING
AND THE ONLY WAY TO MOTIVATE PEOPLE
IS TO COMMUNICATE WITH THEM.

*Never let
an opportunity
pass to say
a kind or
encouraging word
to or about
somebody.*

Let your virtues speak
for themselves,
refuse to talk of another's
vices
and discourage gossip,
it's a waste of time
and can be
extremely destructive.

A SMILE CAN BE REST

TO THE WEARY,

DAYLIGHT TO THE DISCOURAGED,

SUNSHINE TO THE SAD

AND NATURE'S BEST

ANTIDOTE FOR TROUBLE.

*Obstacles are those frightful things you see when you take your eyes off your **goal**.*

Don't ever expect loyalty –
you will be disappointed.

Don't ever demand loyalty –
you won't get it.

*Loyalty is earned
by your actions.*

In business
people take
different roads
to achieve success –
just because they are
not on your road
doesn't mean that
they've got lost.

Experience is
the hardest kind
of teacher,
it gives you
the test first
the lesson
and the lesson
afterwards…

Doing things by halves can be worthless because it may be the other half that counts.

CHILDREN HAVE MORE NEED OF ROLE MODELS THAN OF CRITICS.

Worrying about **what's** right is always more important than worrying about **who's** right.

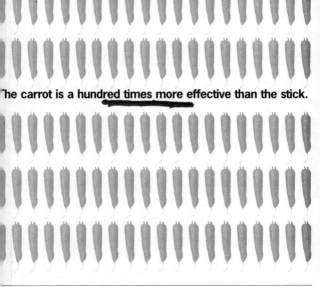

The carrot is a hundred times more effective than the stick.

FREE
Subscribe to our free Thought for the Day at:
http://www.denny.co.uk/content/training-resources/thought-for-the-day.php

Visit our website: **www.denny.co.uk**
Email: **success@denny.co.uk**
Telephone: +44 (0) **1608 812424**
Fax: + 44 (0) **1608 651638**

Mail: **RDG**
Cotswold Business Village
Moreton-in-Marsh
Gloucestershire
GL56 0JQ
United Kingdom

Visit the website: **www.denny.co.uk**